The Glory of TOADS Coloring Book

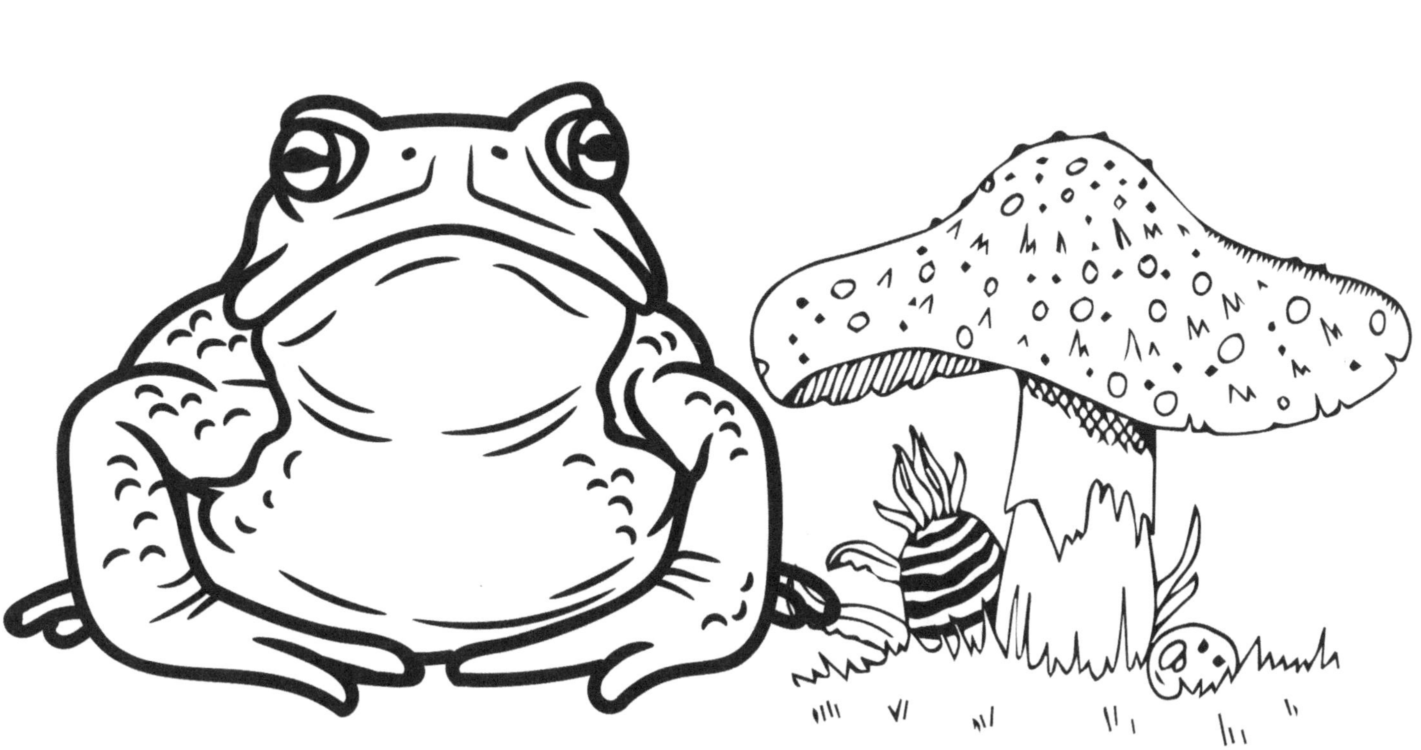

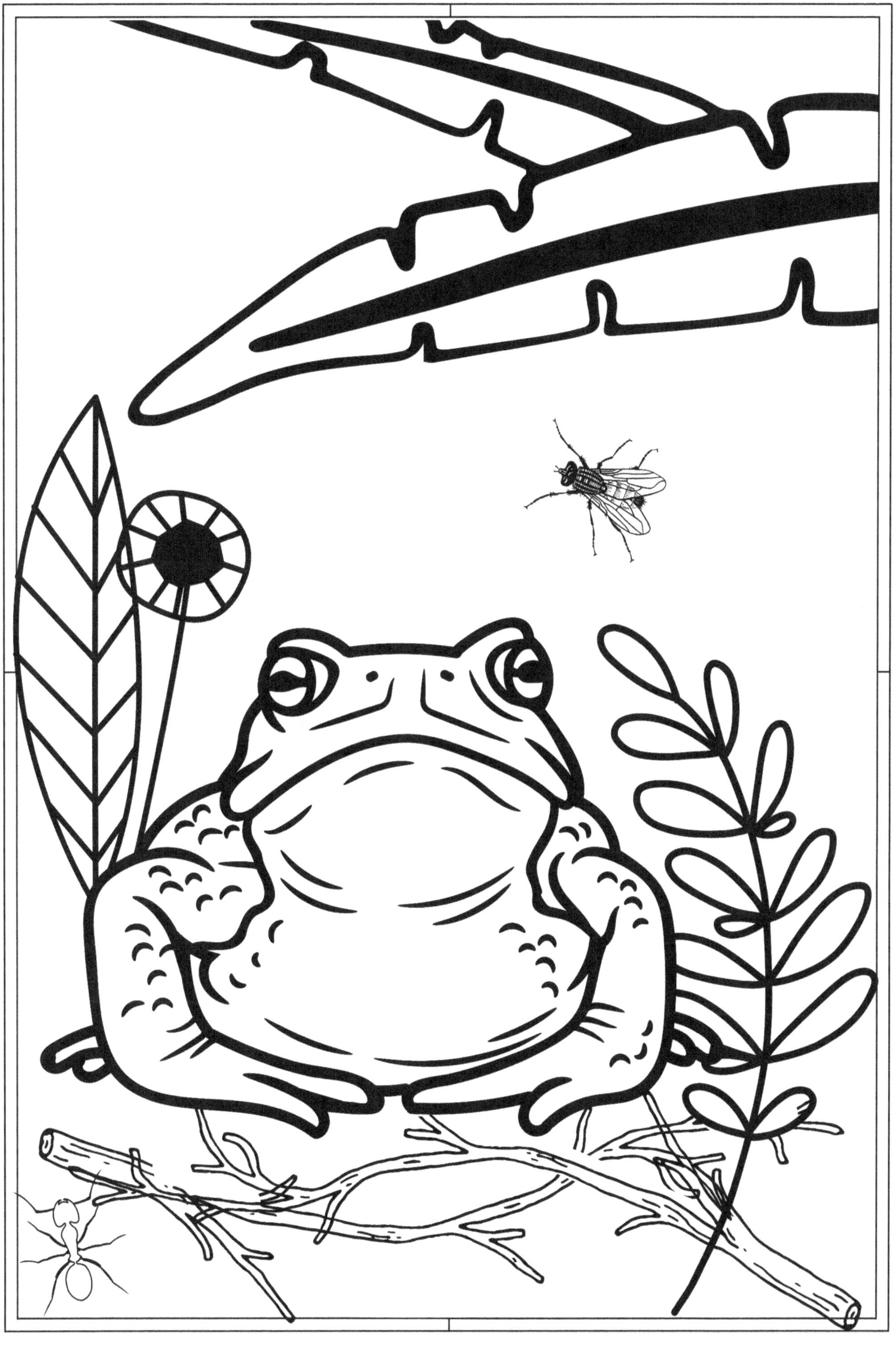

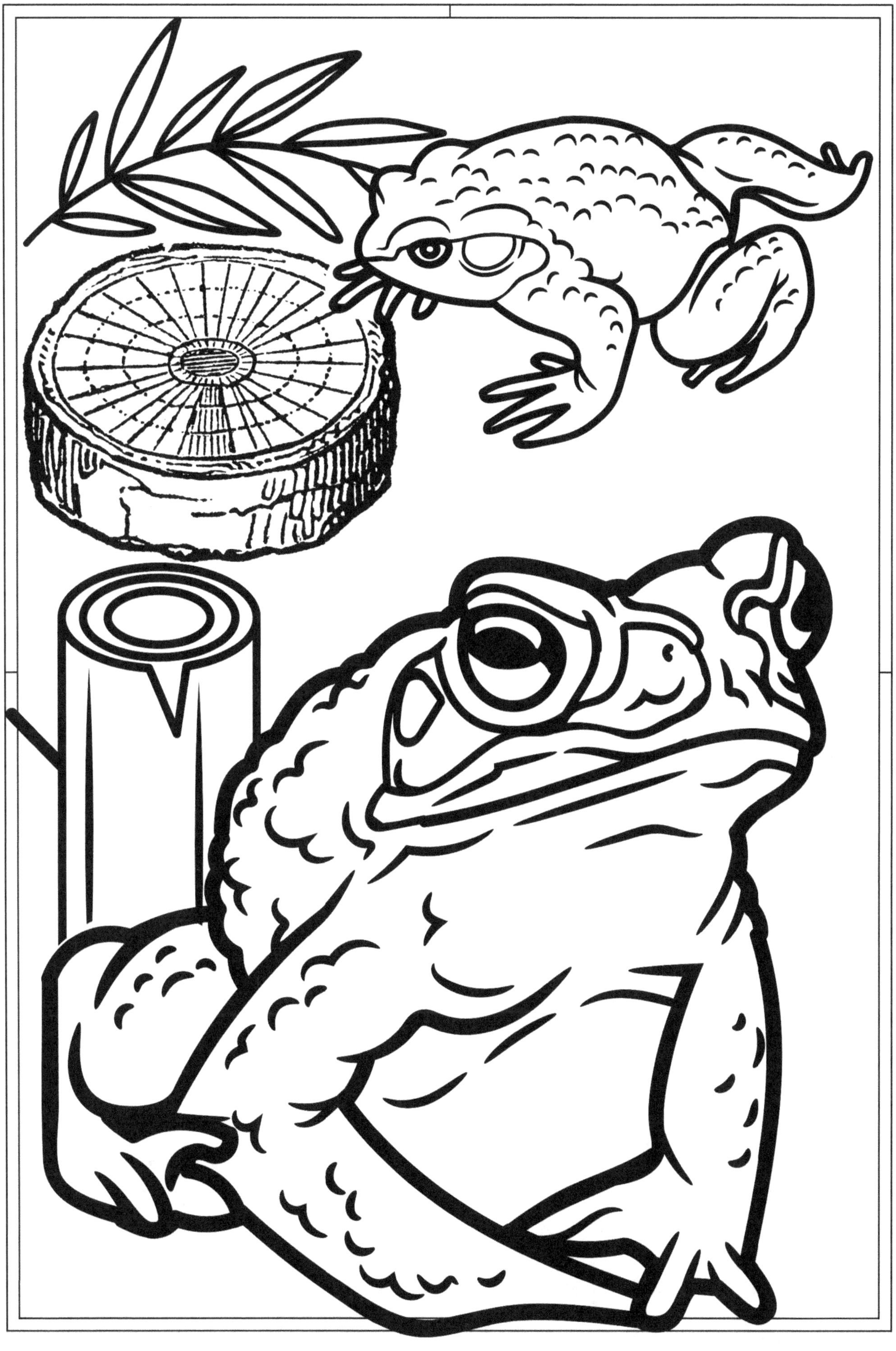

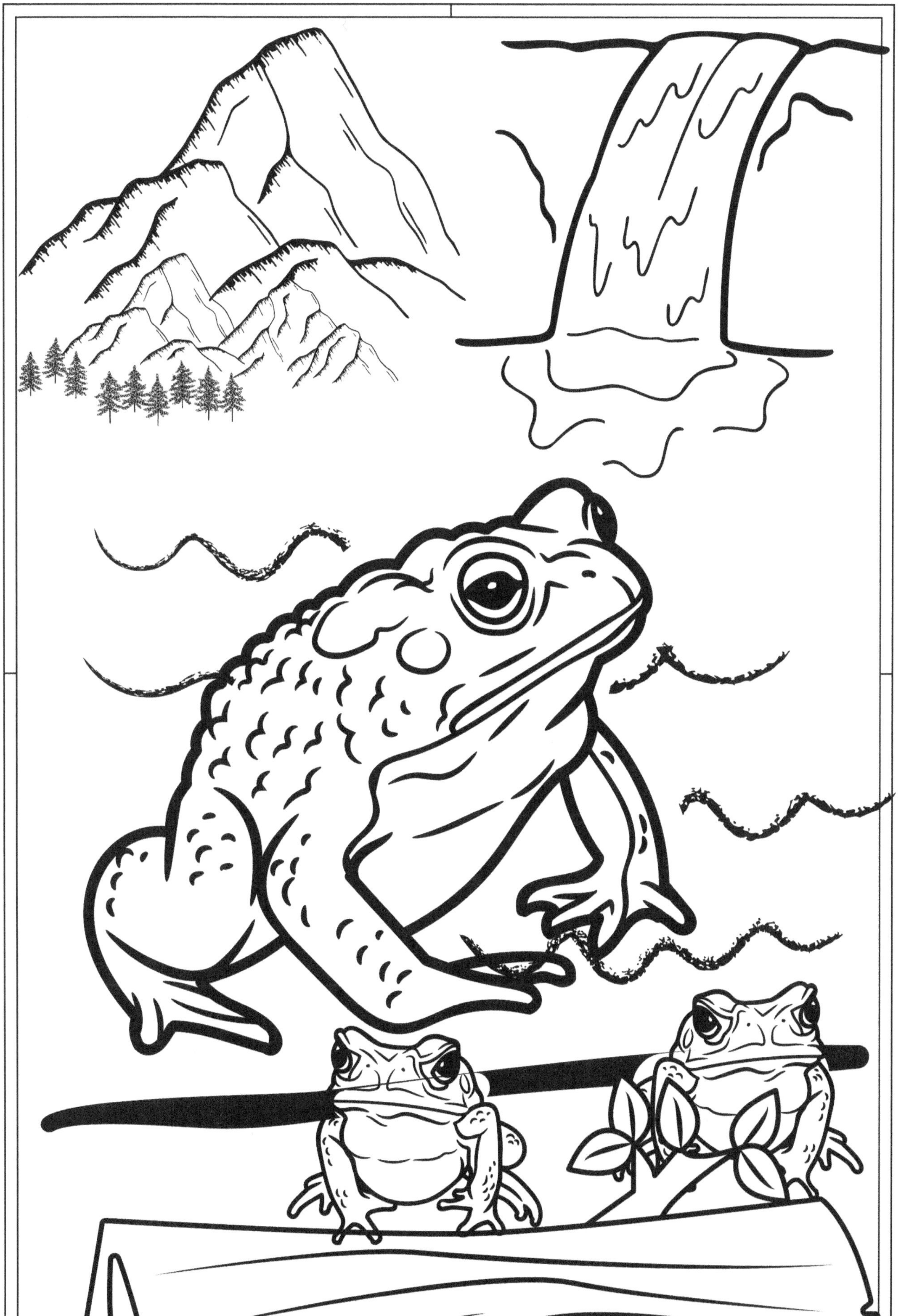

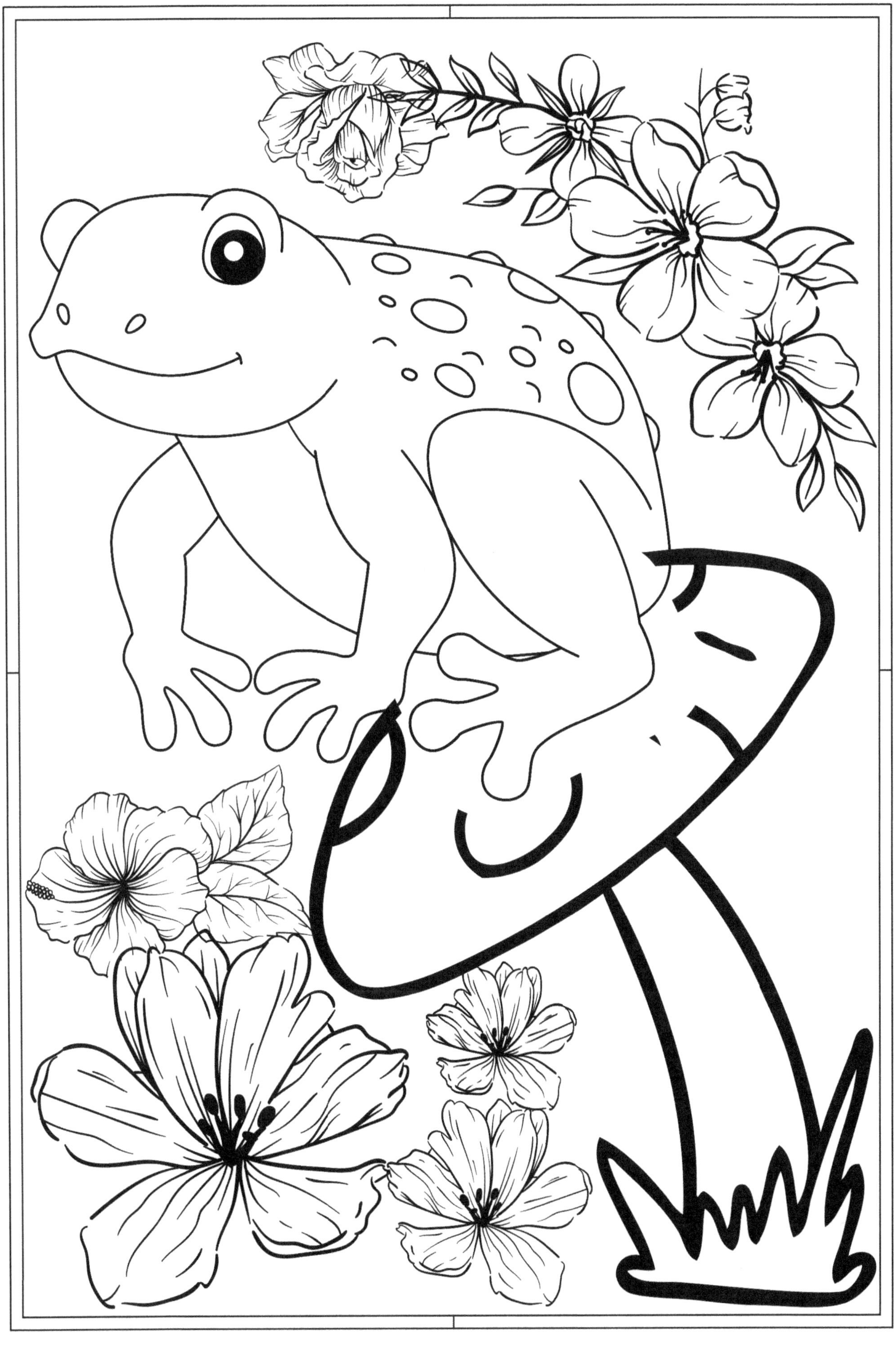

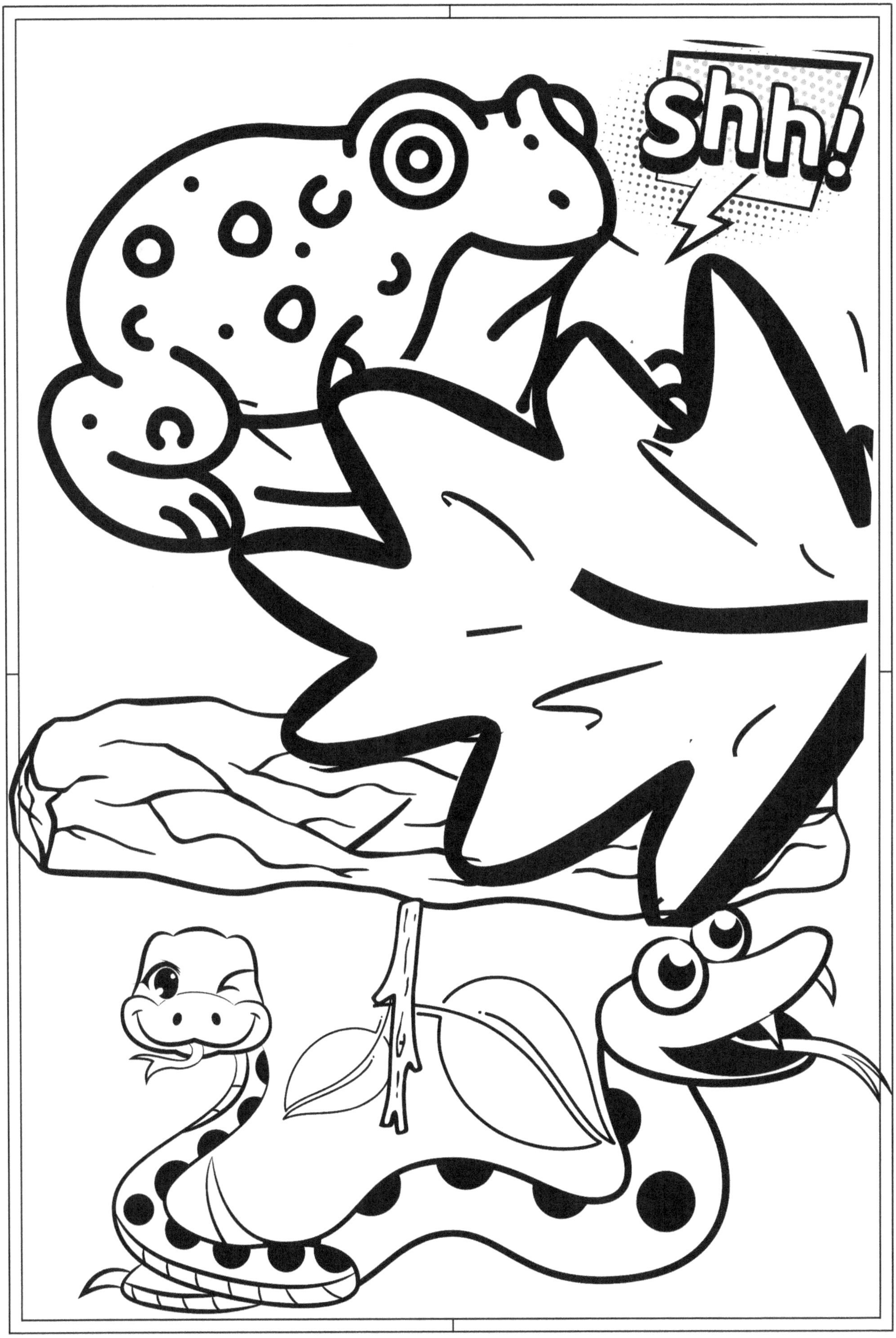
Shh!

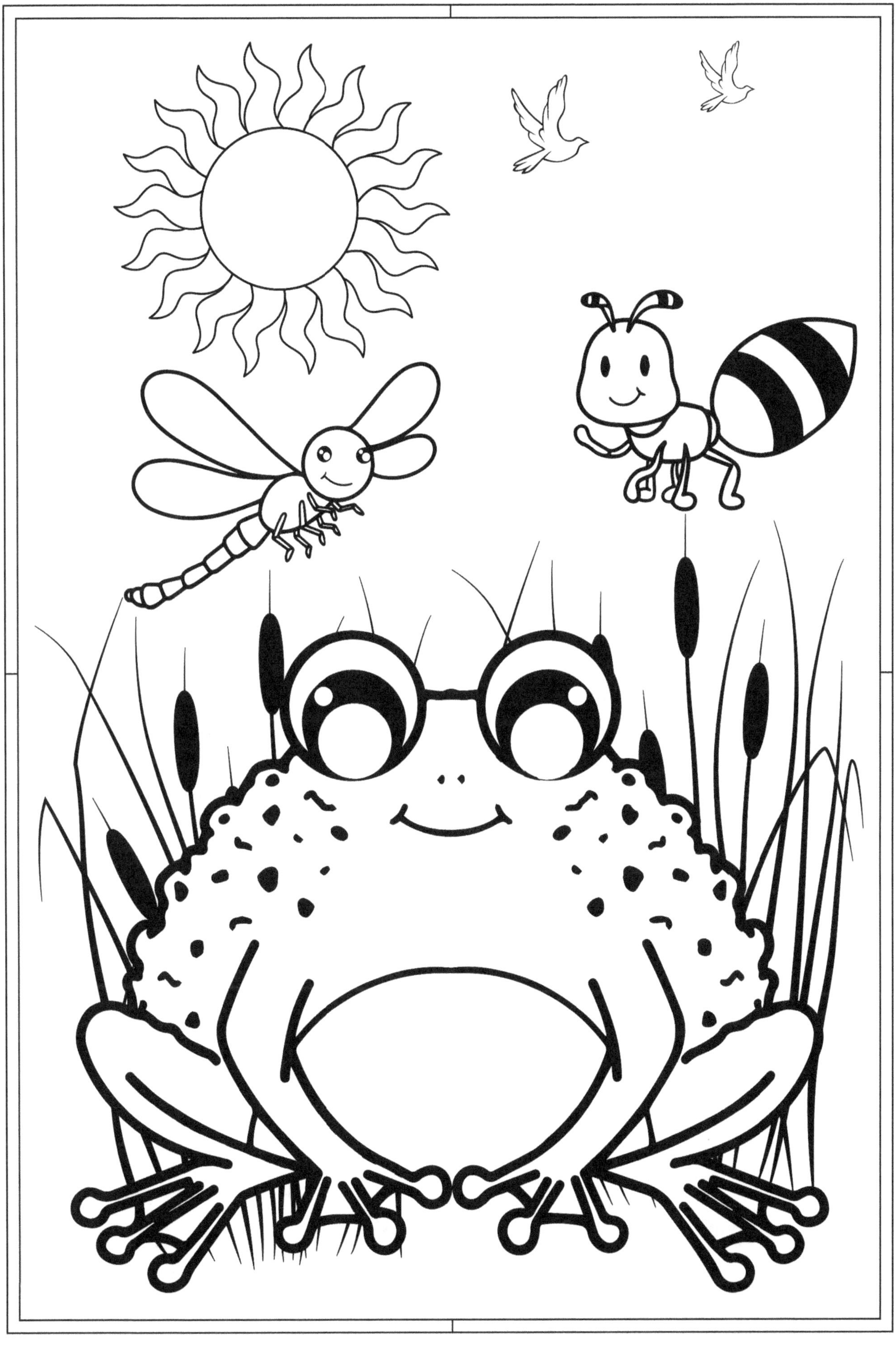

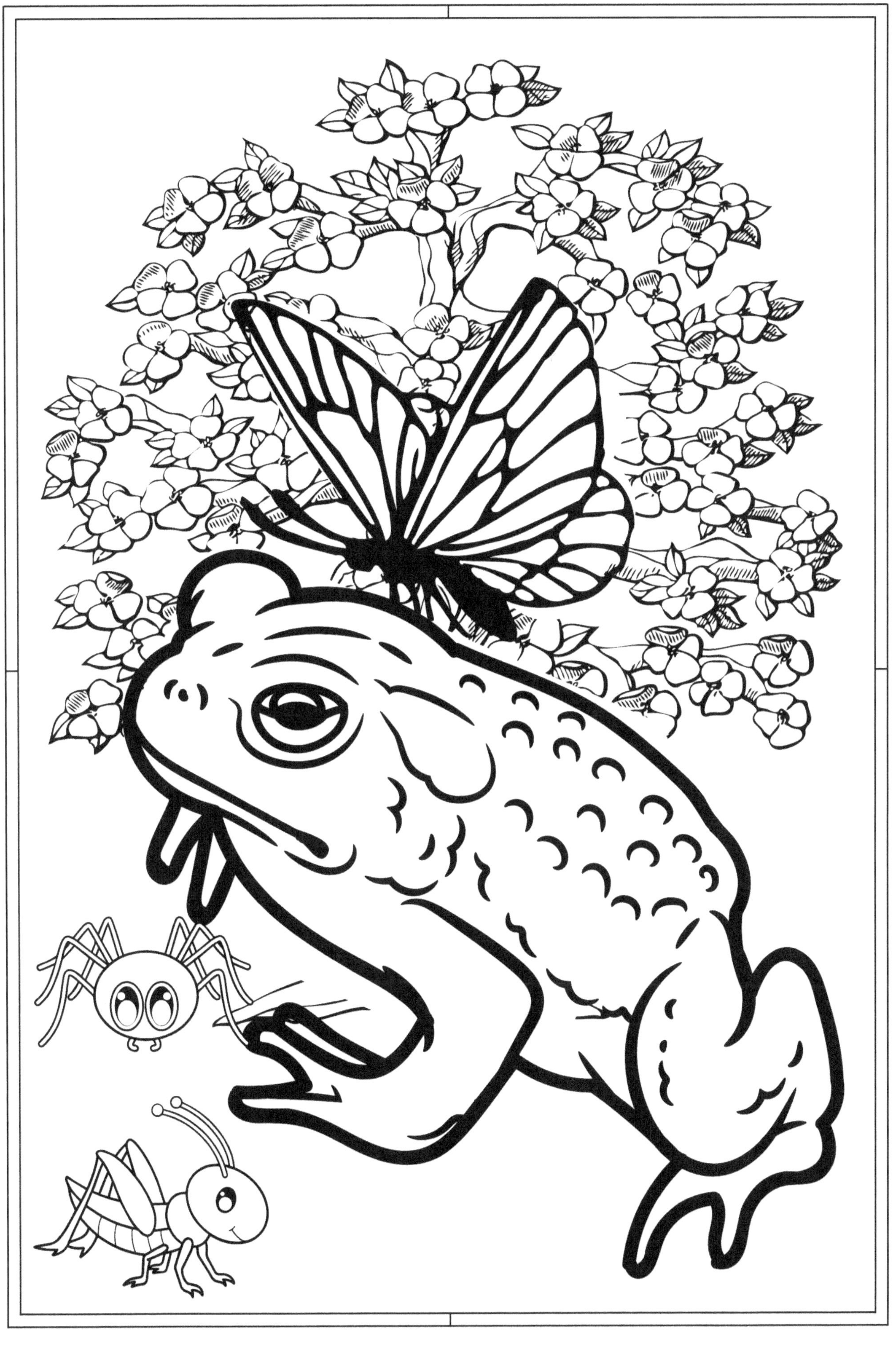

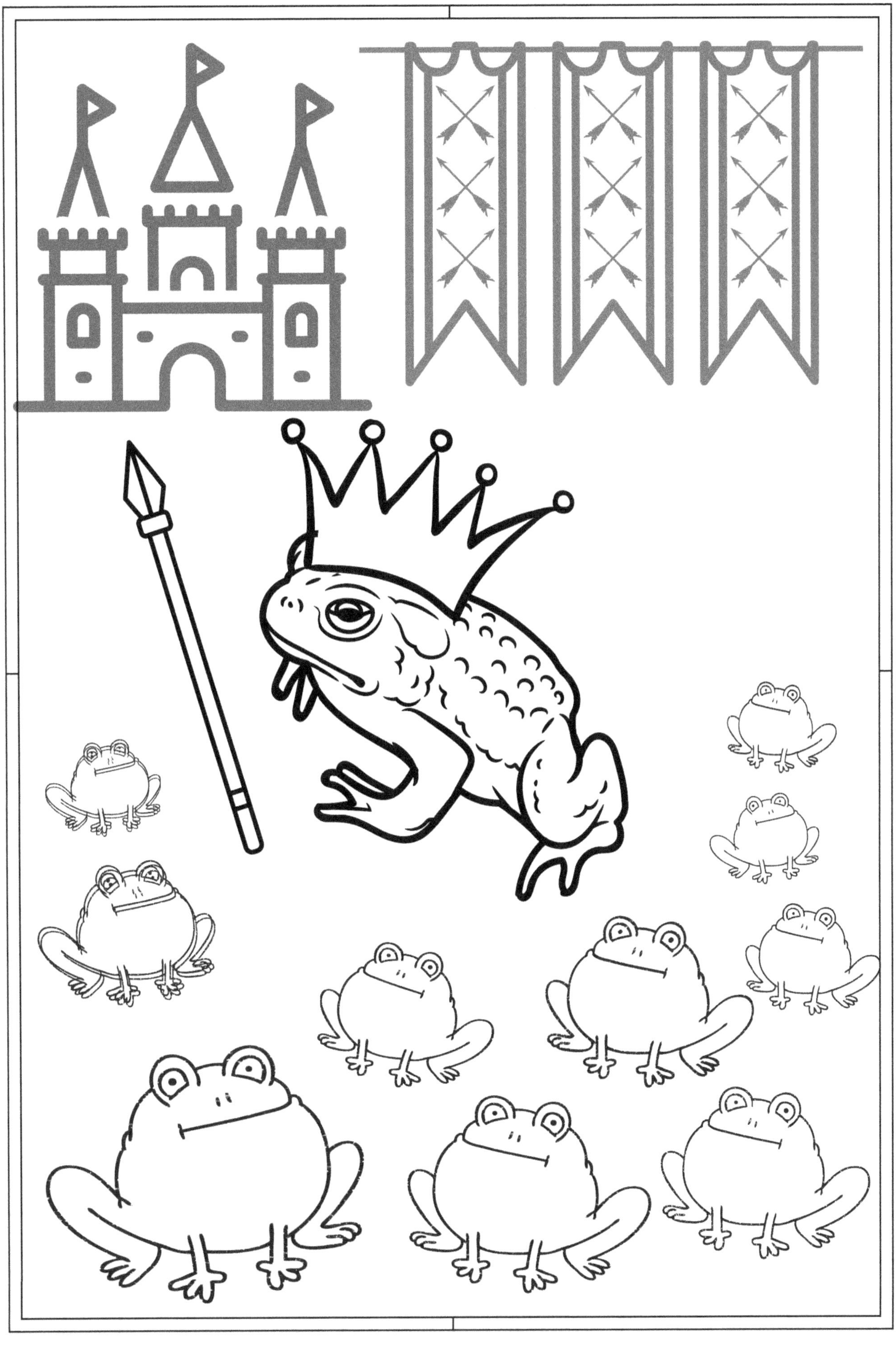

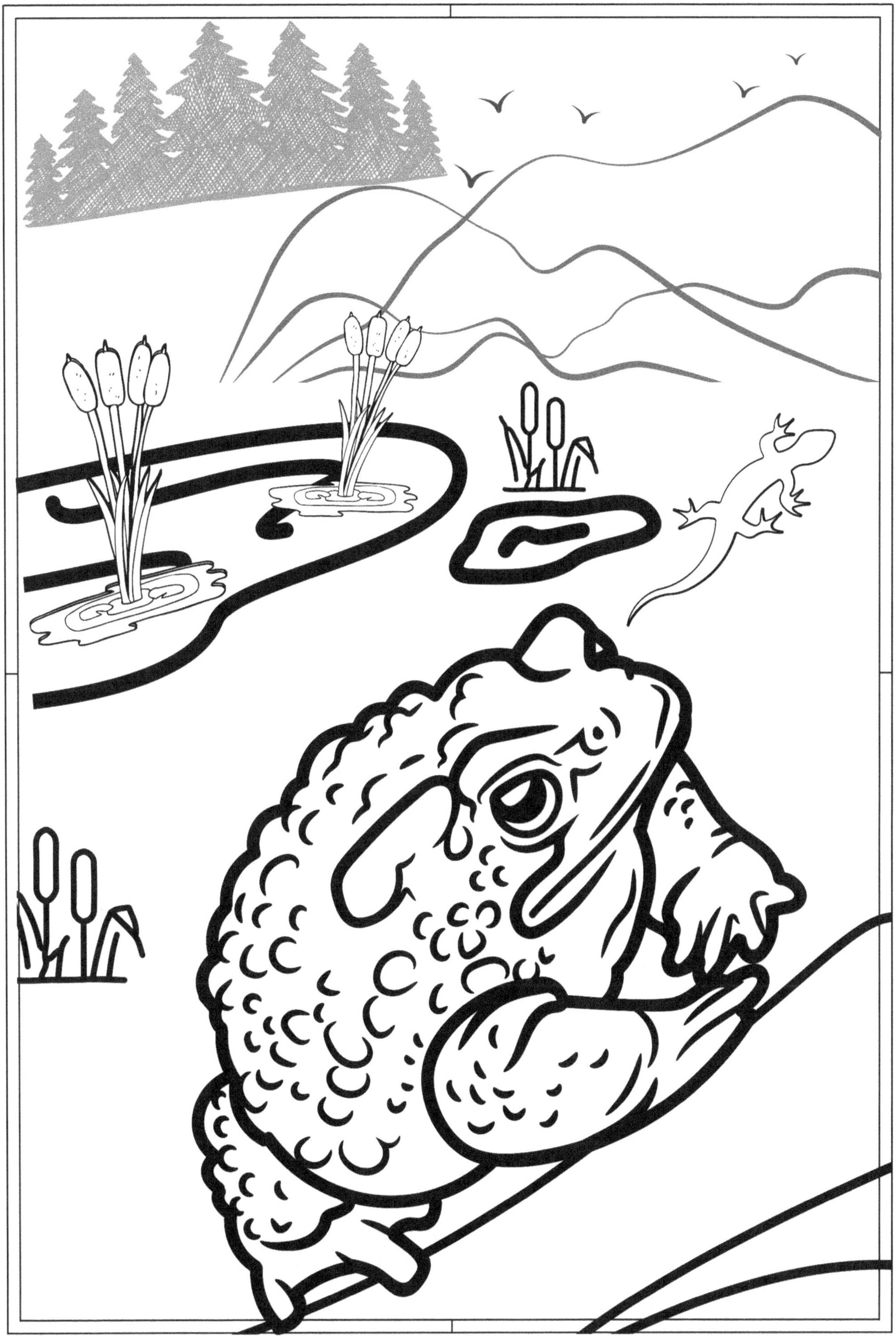

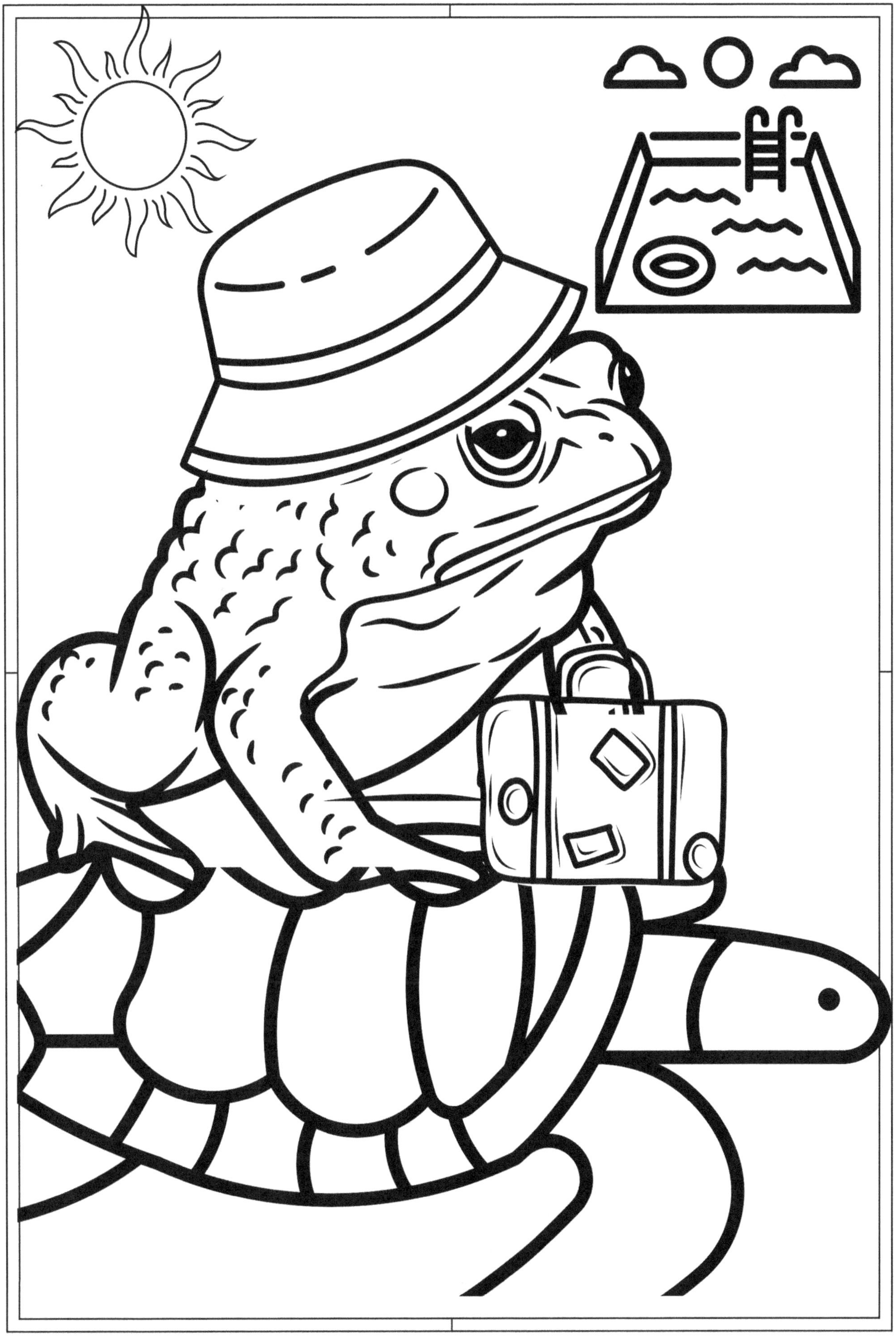

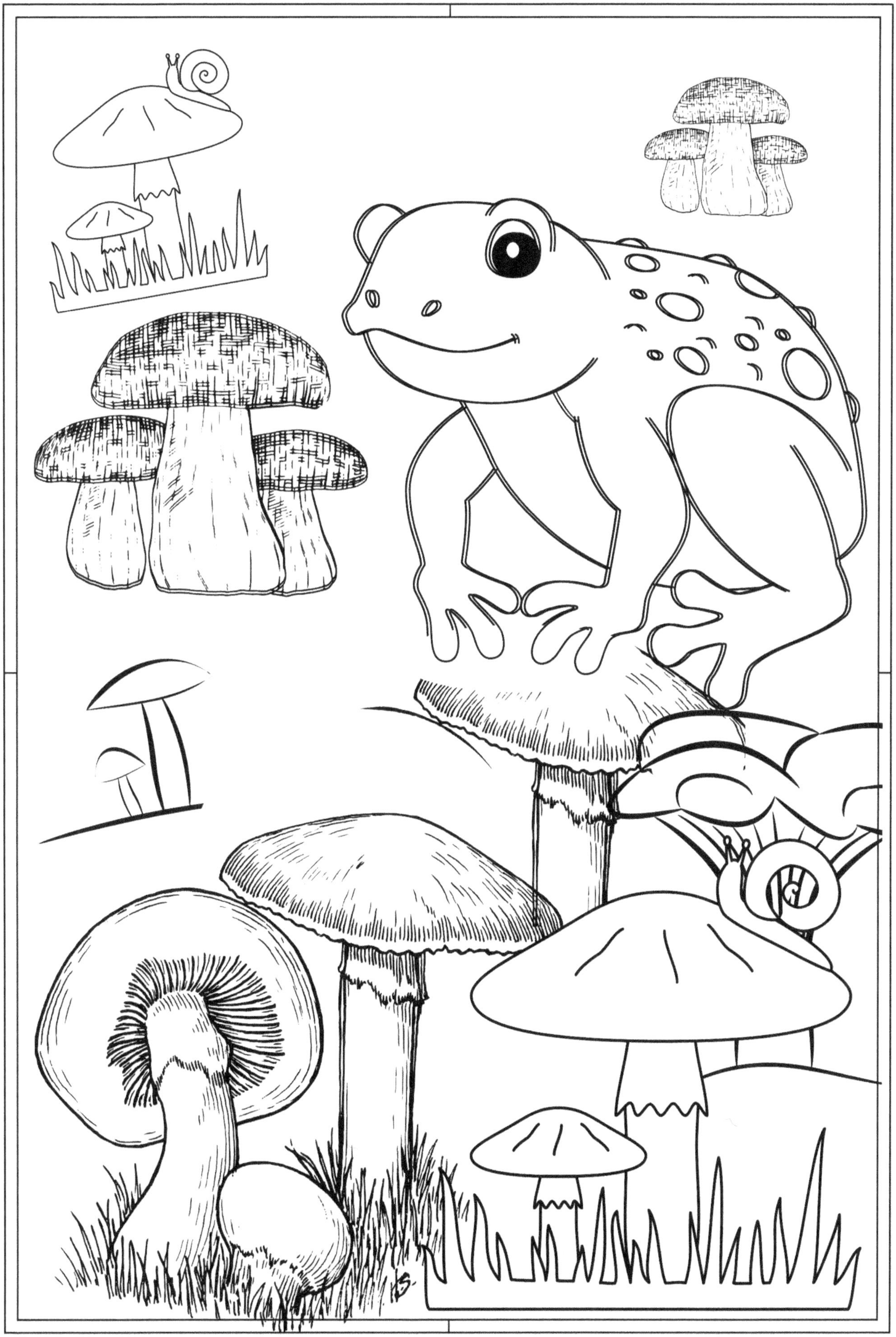

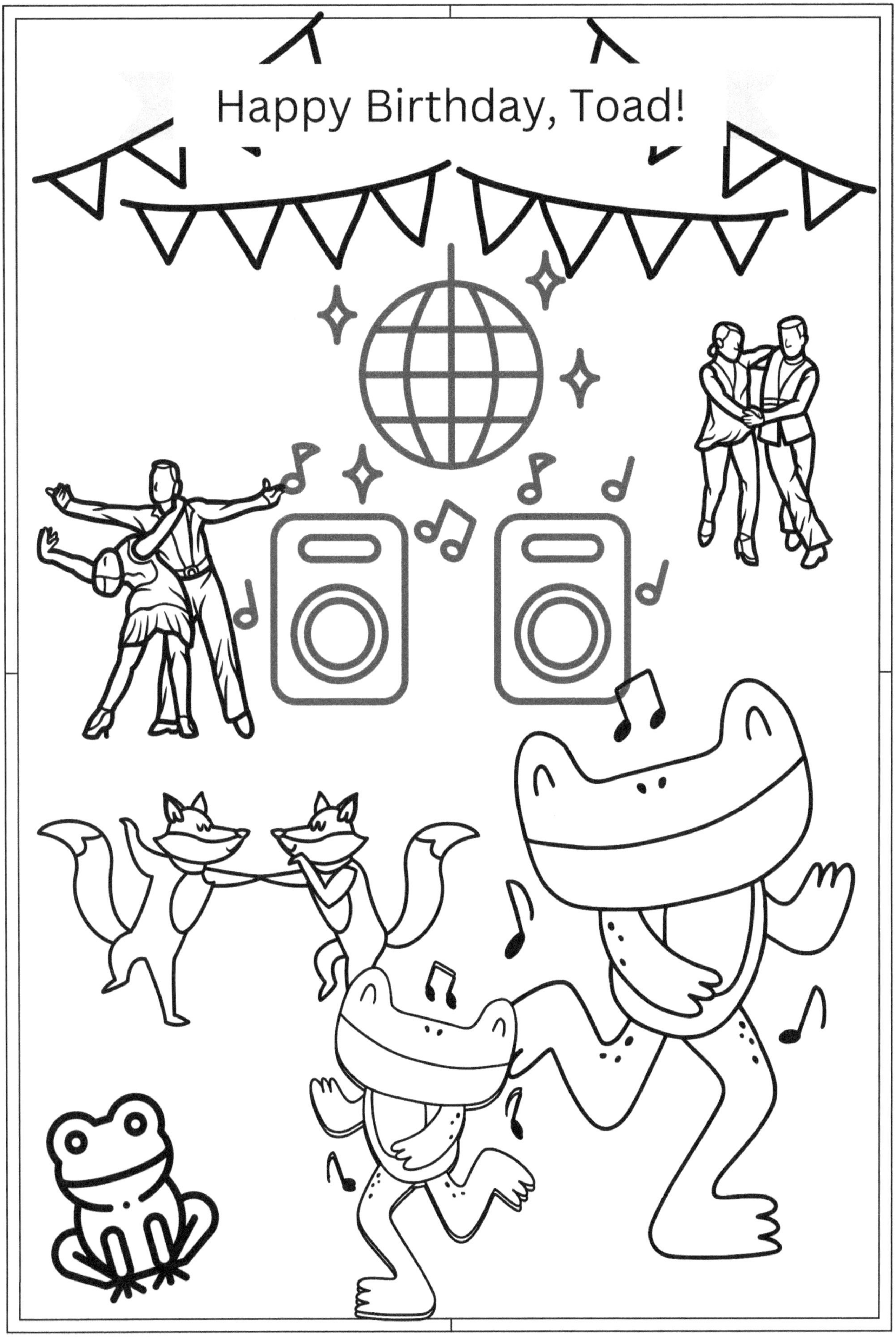
Happy Birthday, Toad!

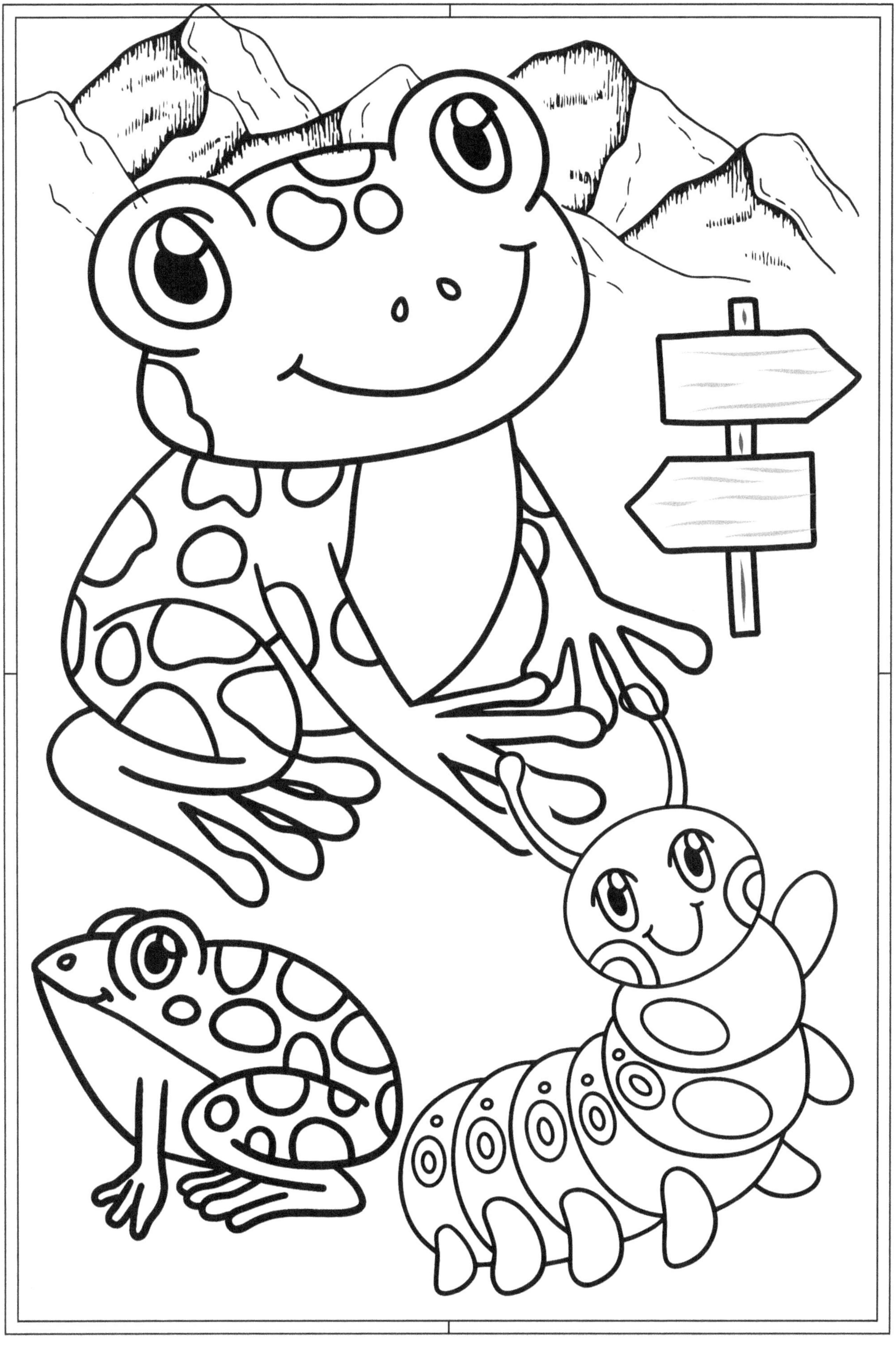

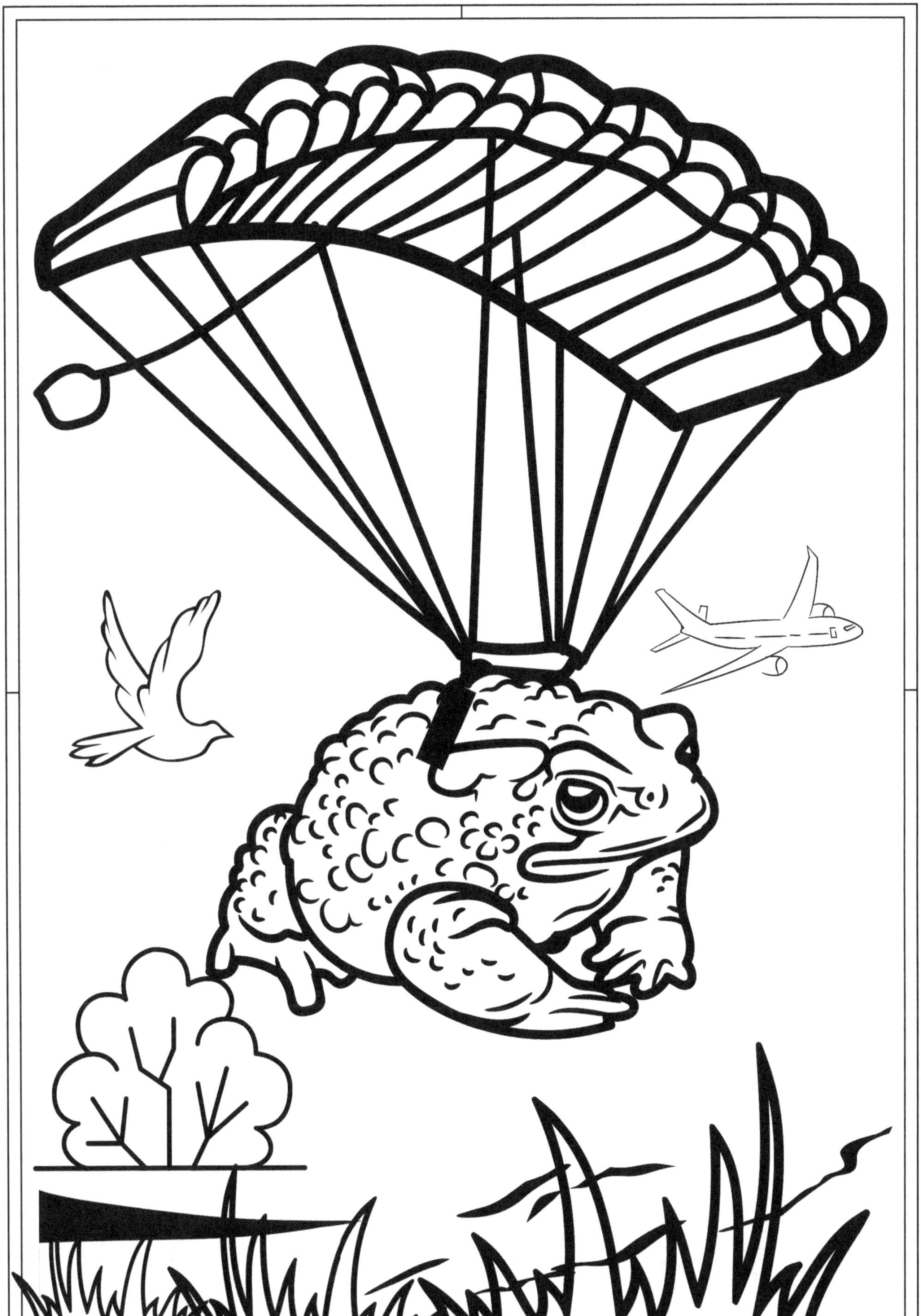

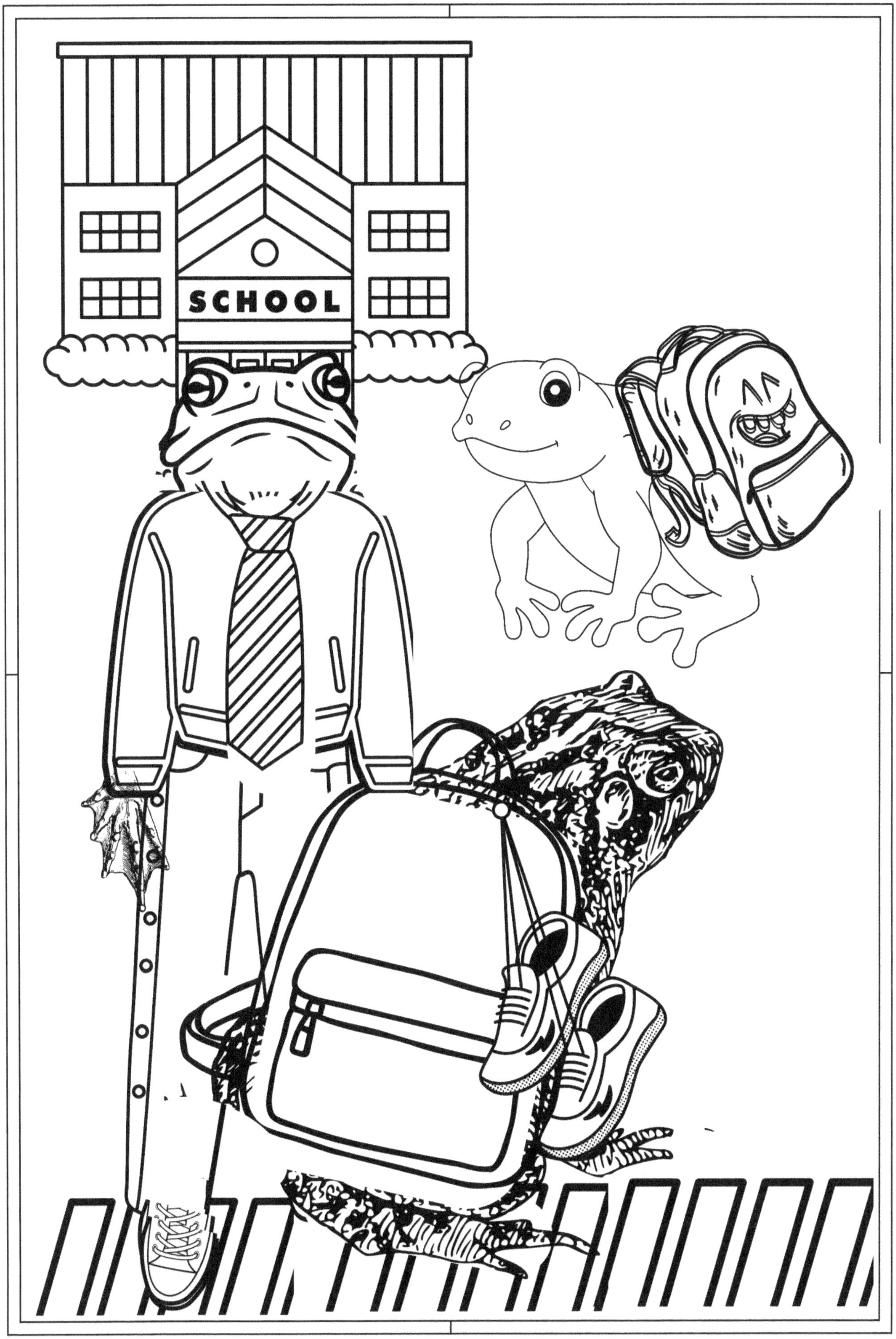
SCHOOL

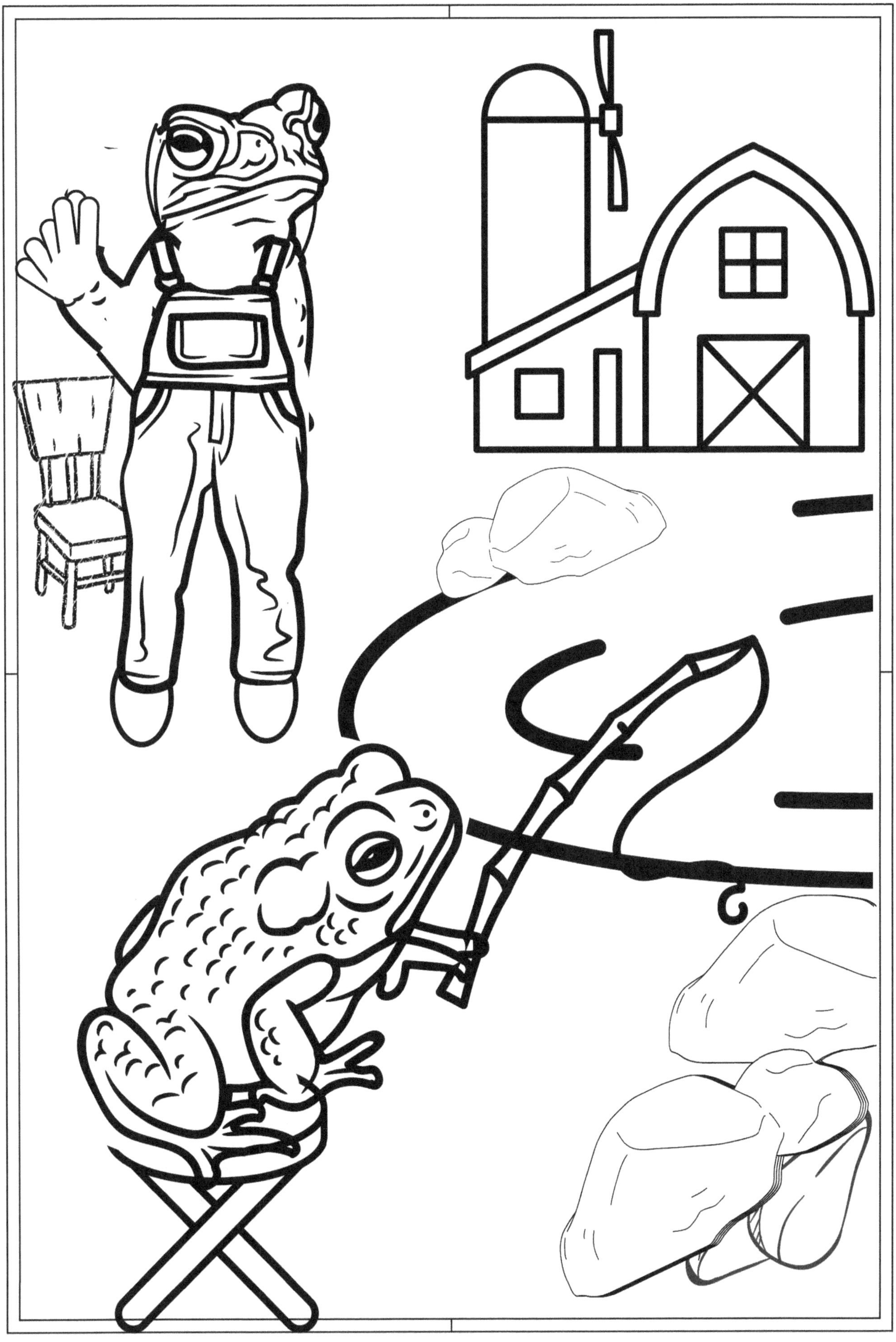

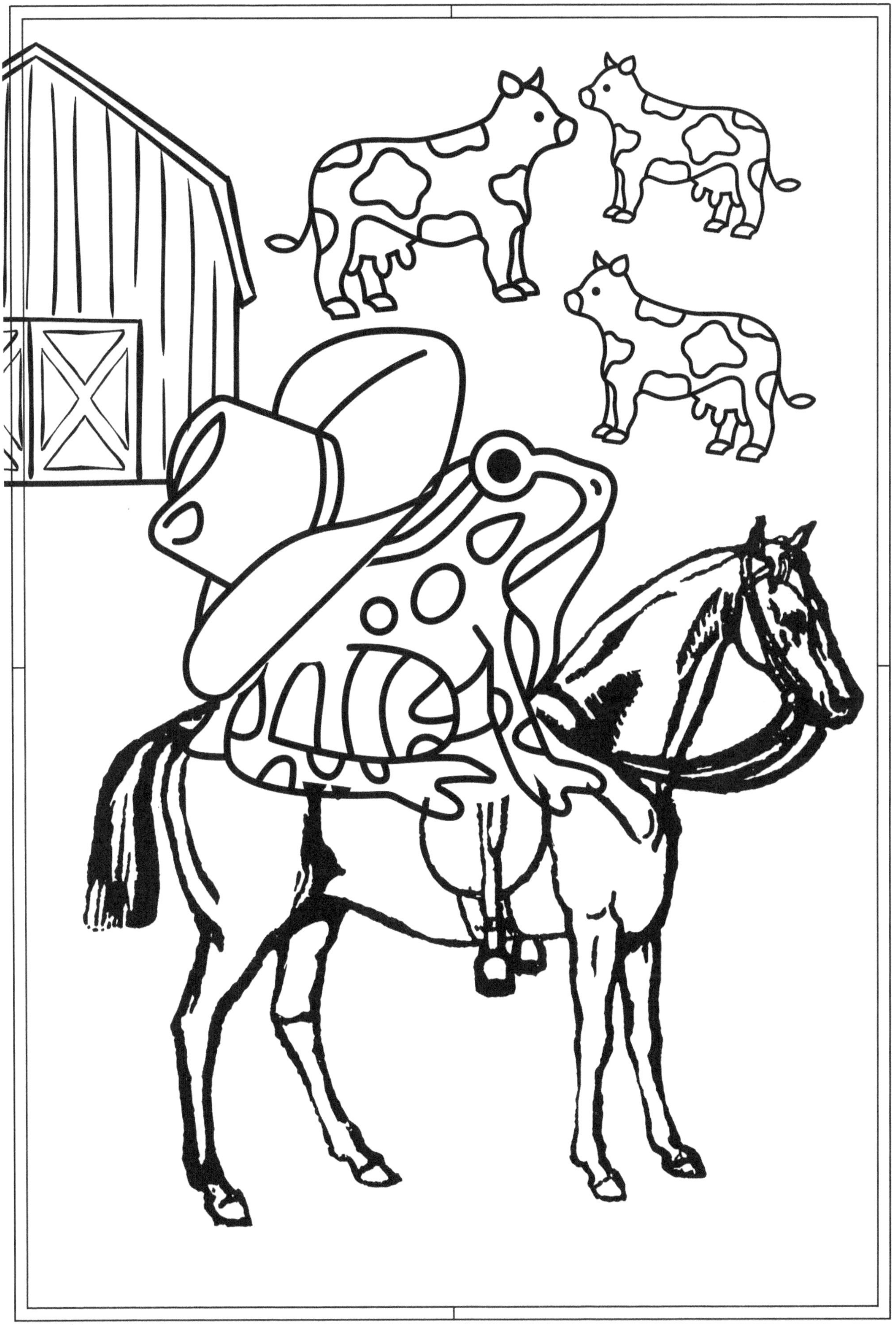

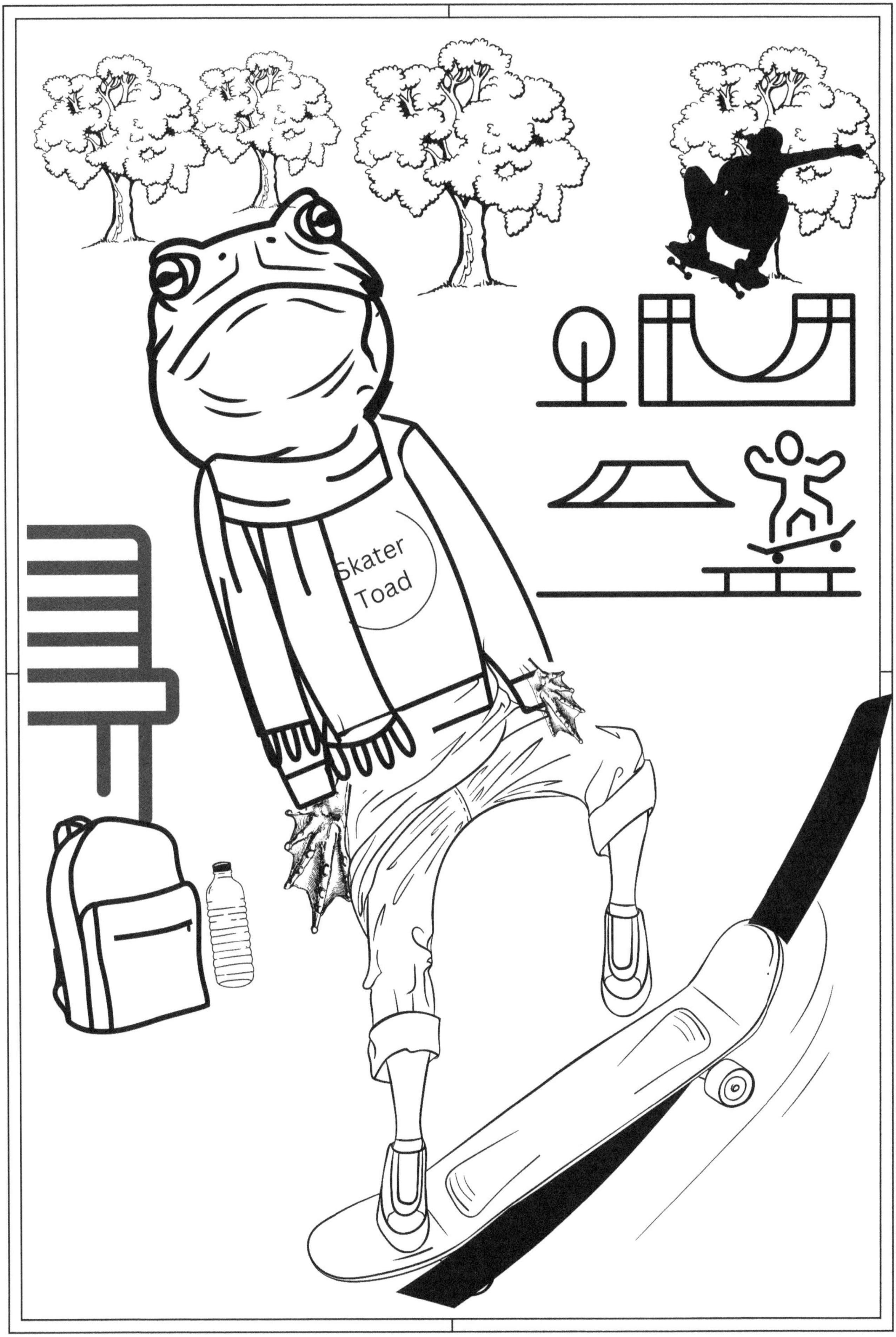
Skater
Toad

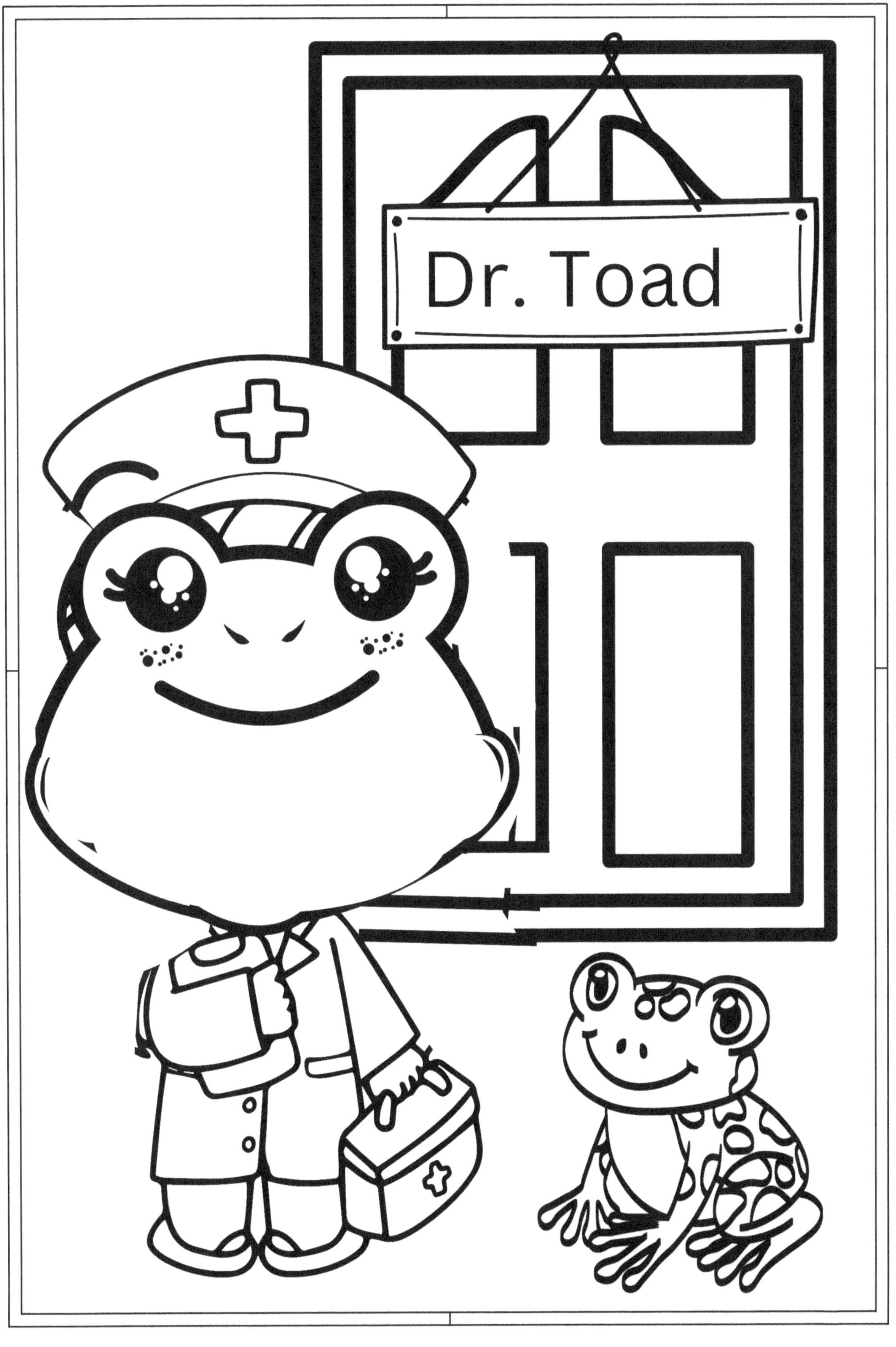
Dr. Toad

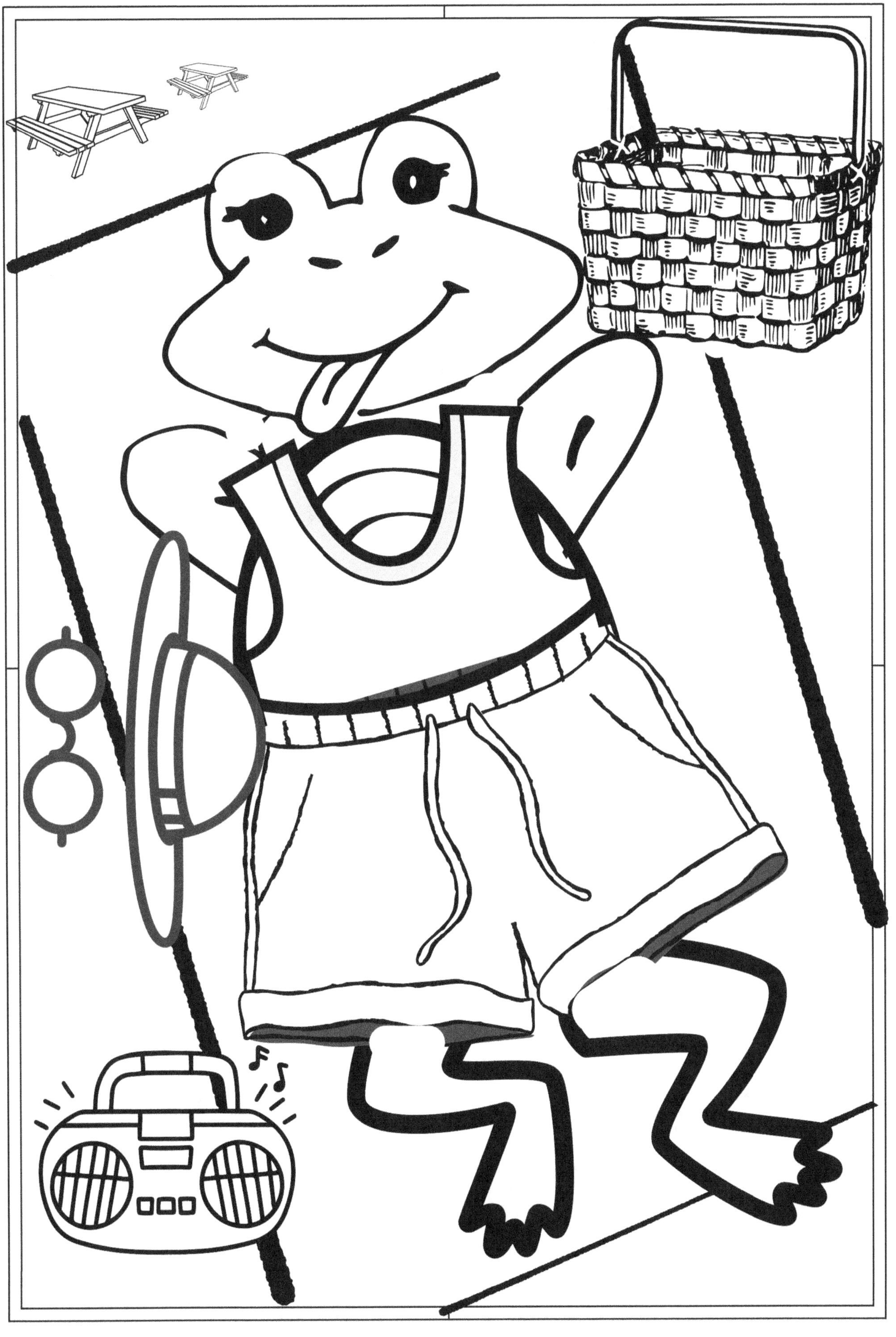

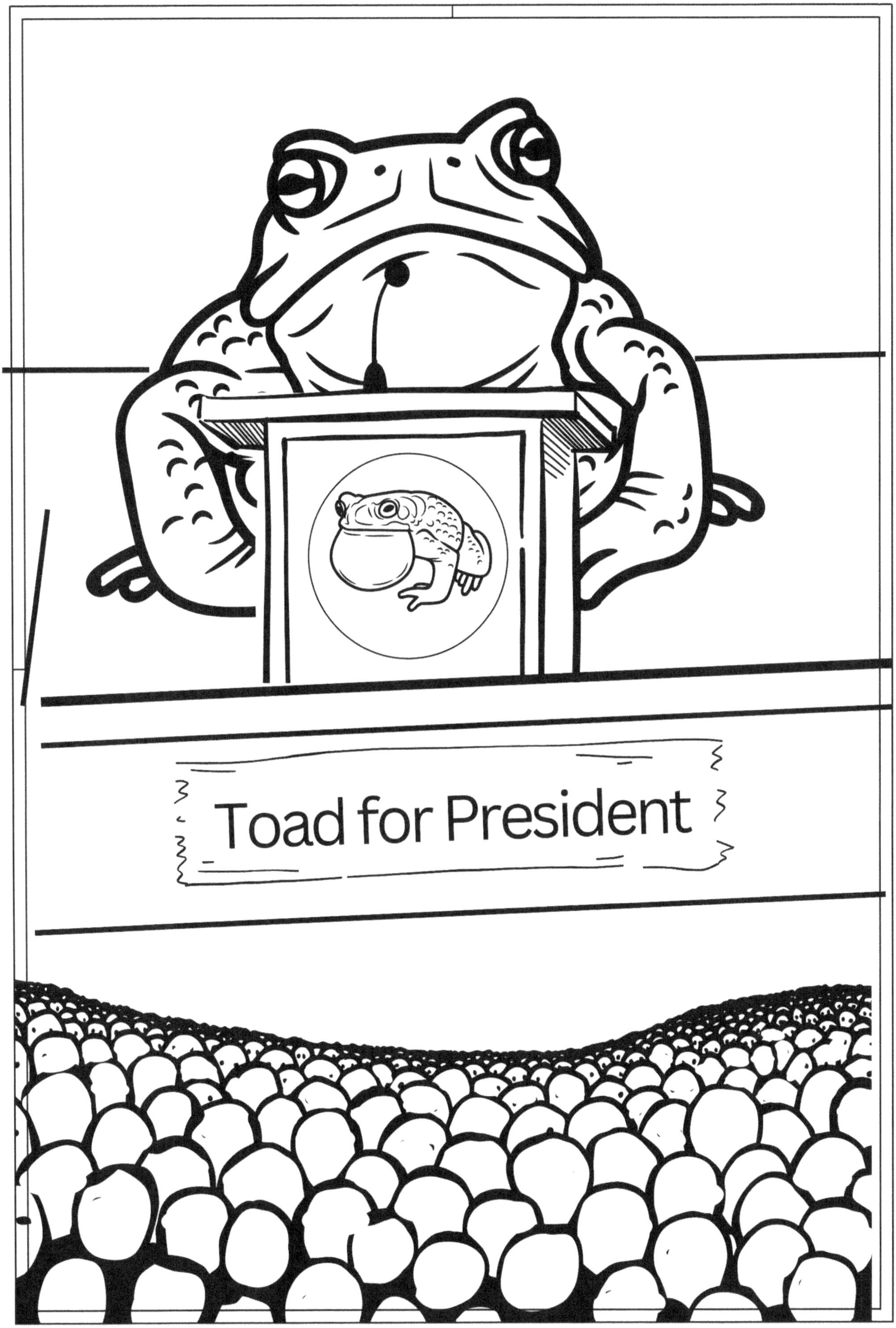
Toad for President

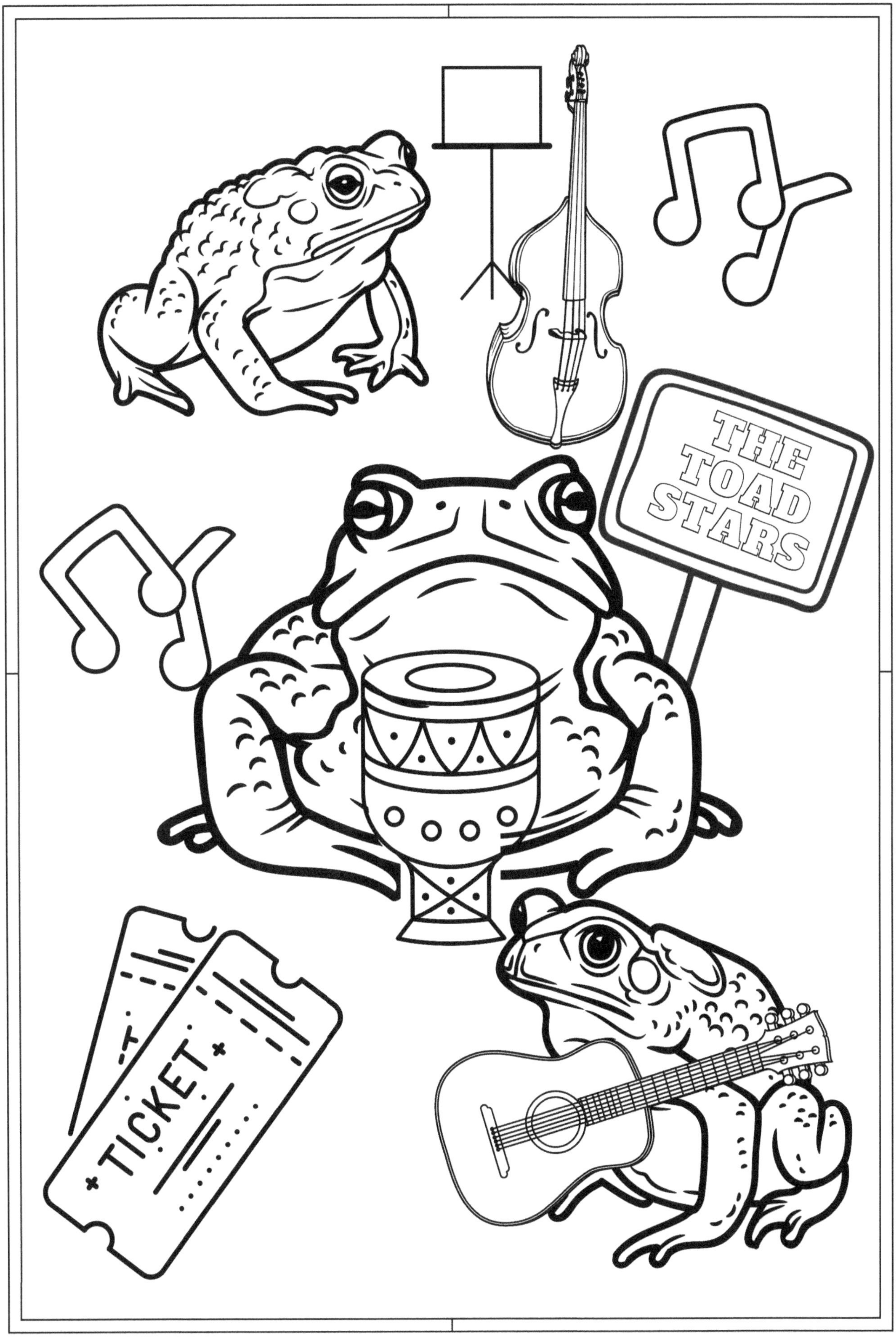
THE
TOAD
STARS
TICKET
TICKET

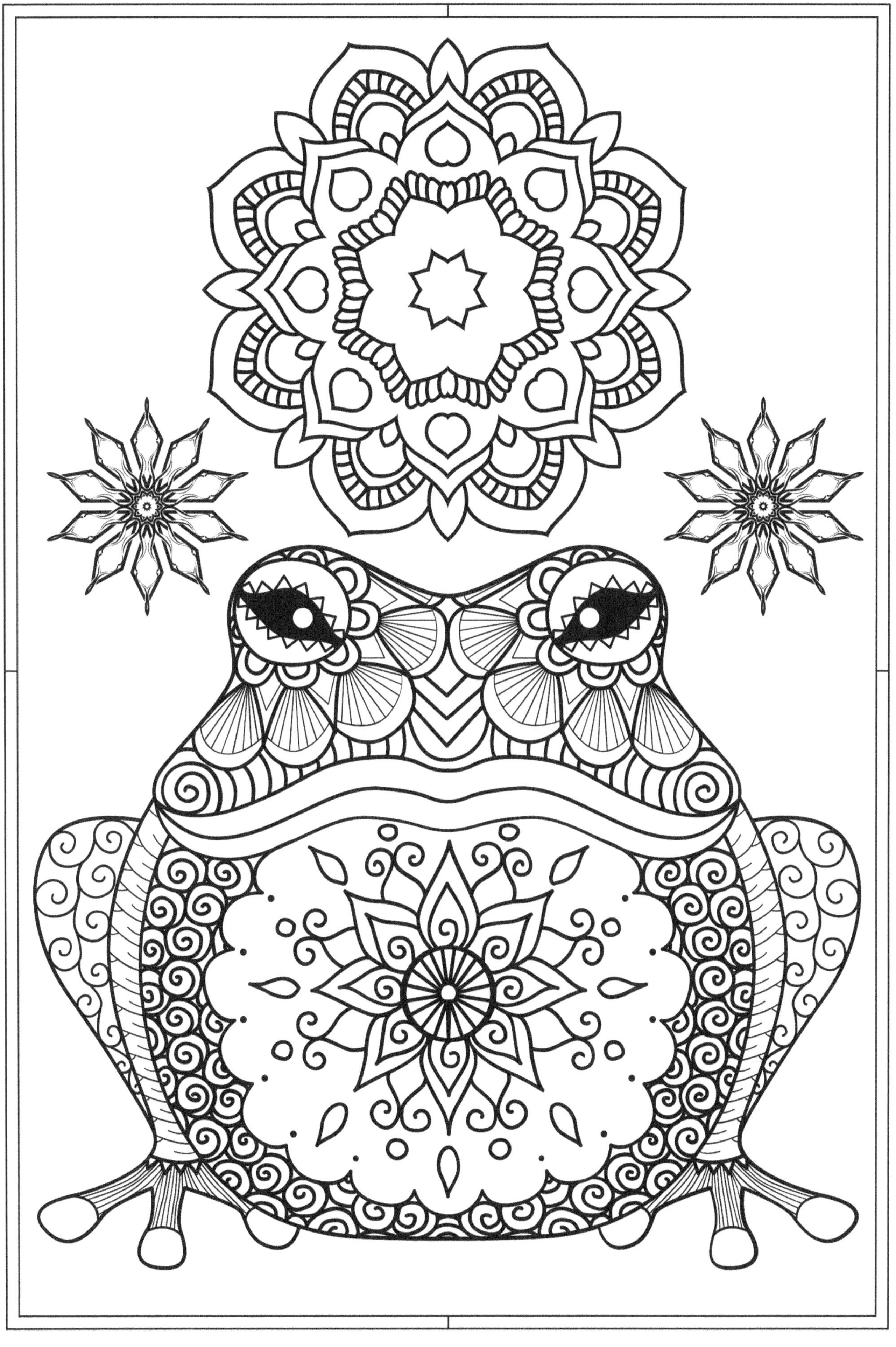

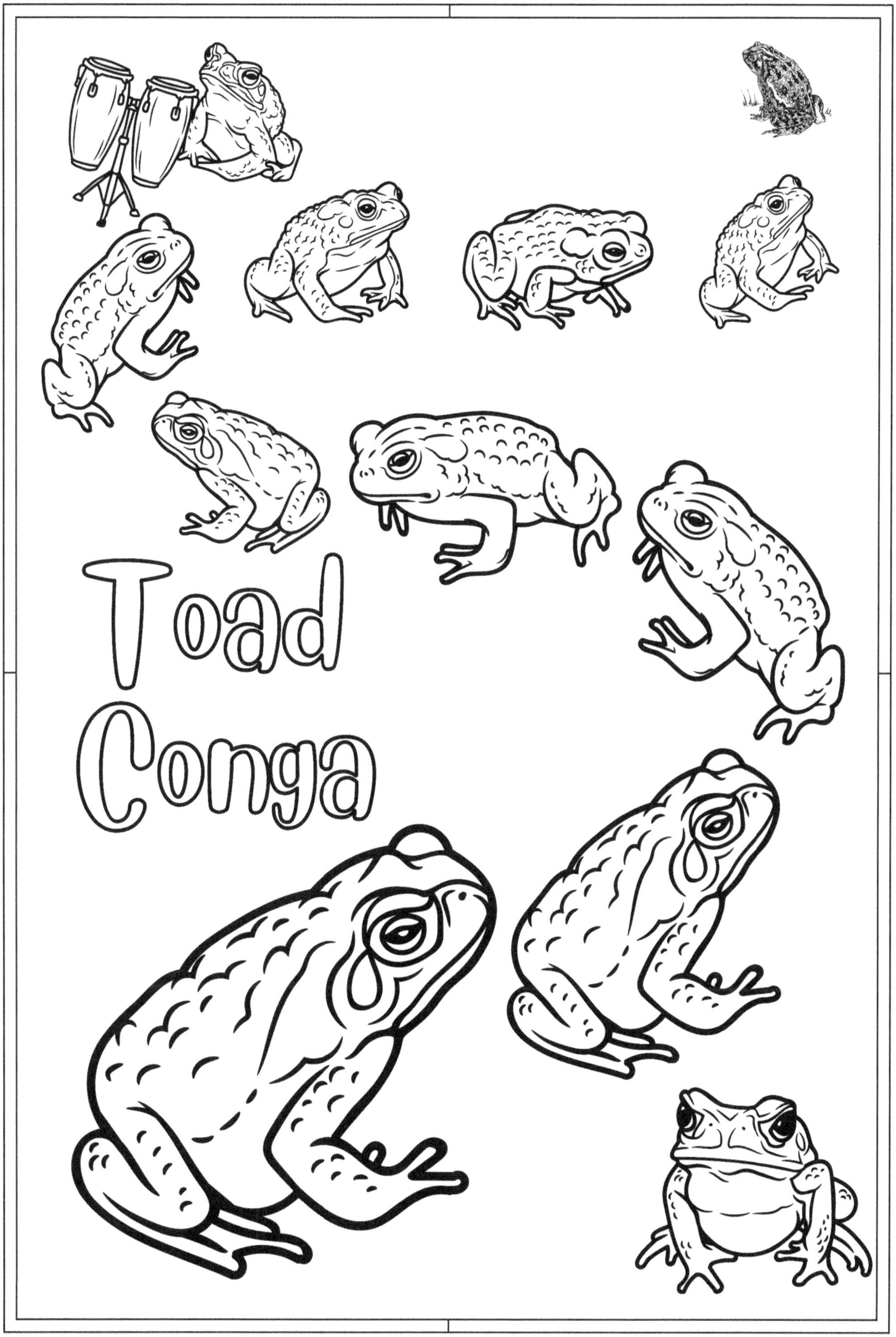
Toad
Conga

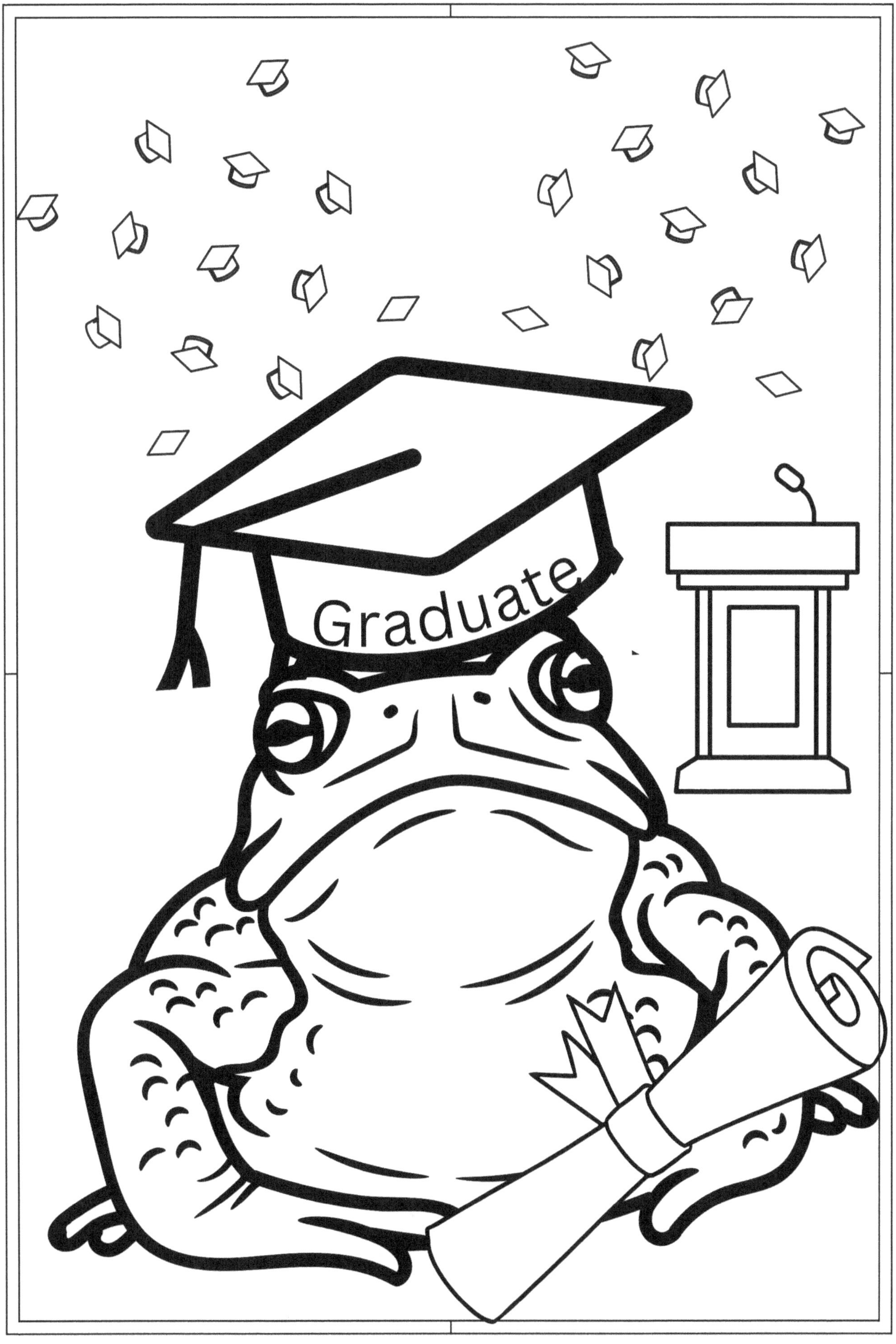
Graduate

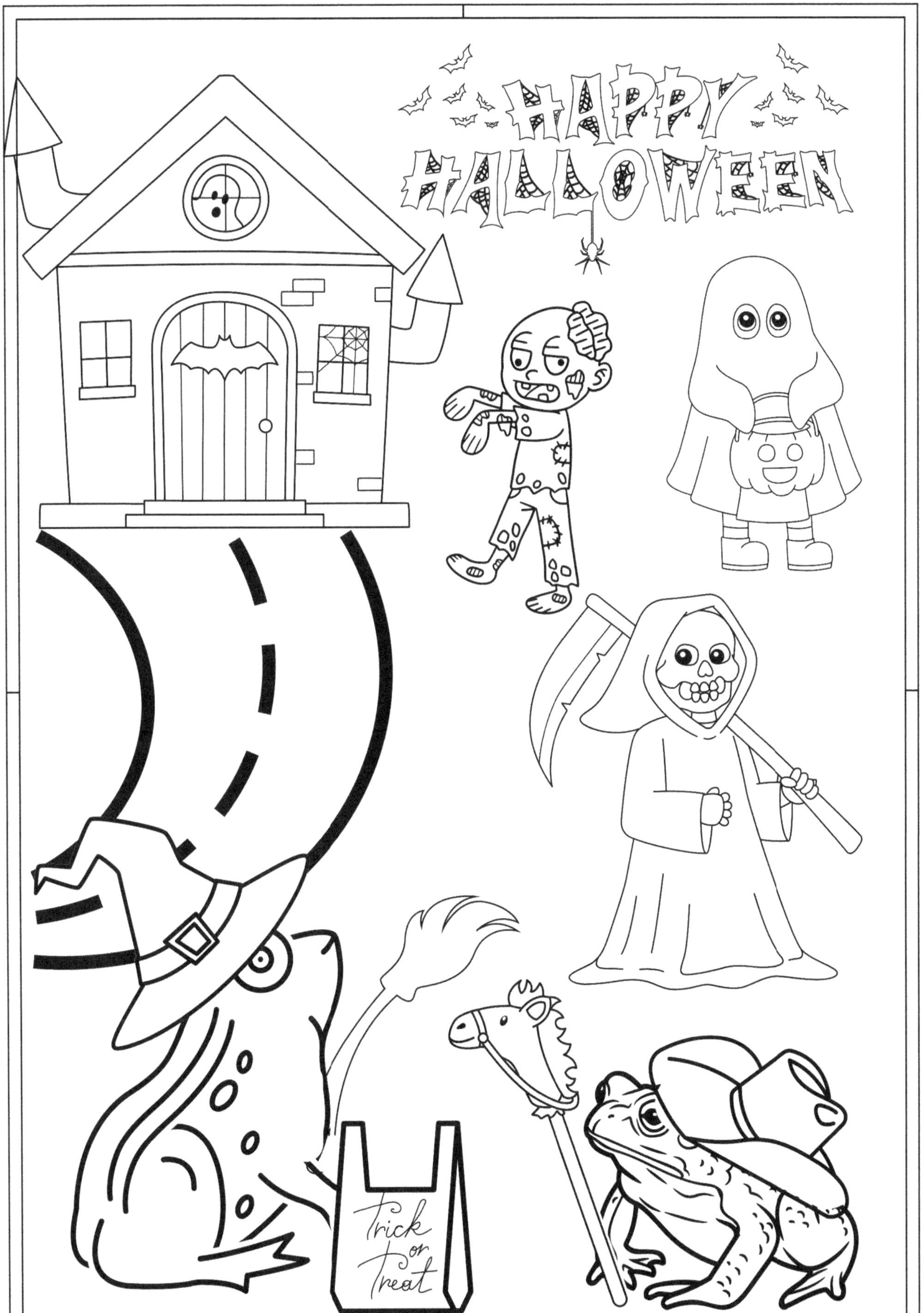
HAPPY
HALLOWEEN
Trick or Treat

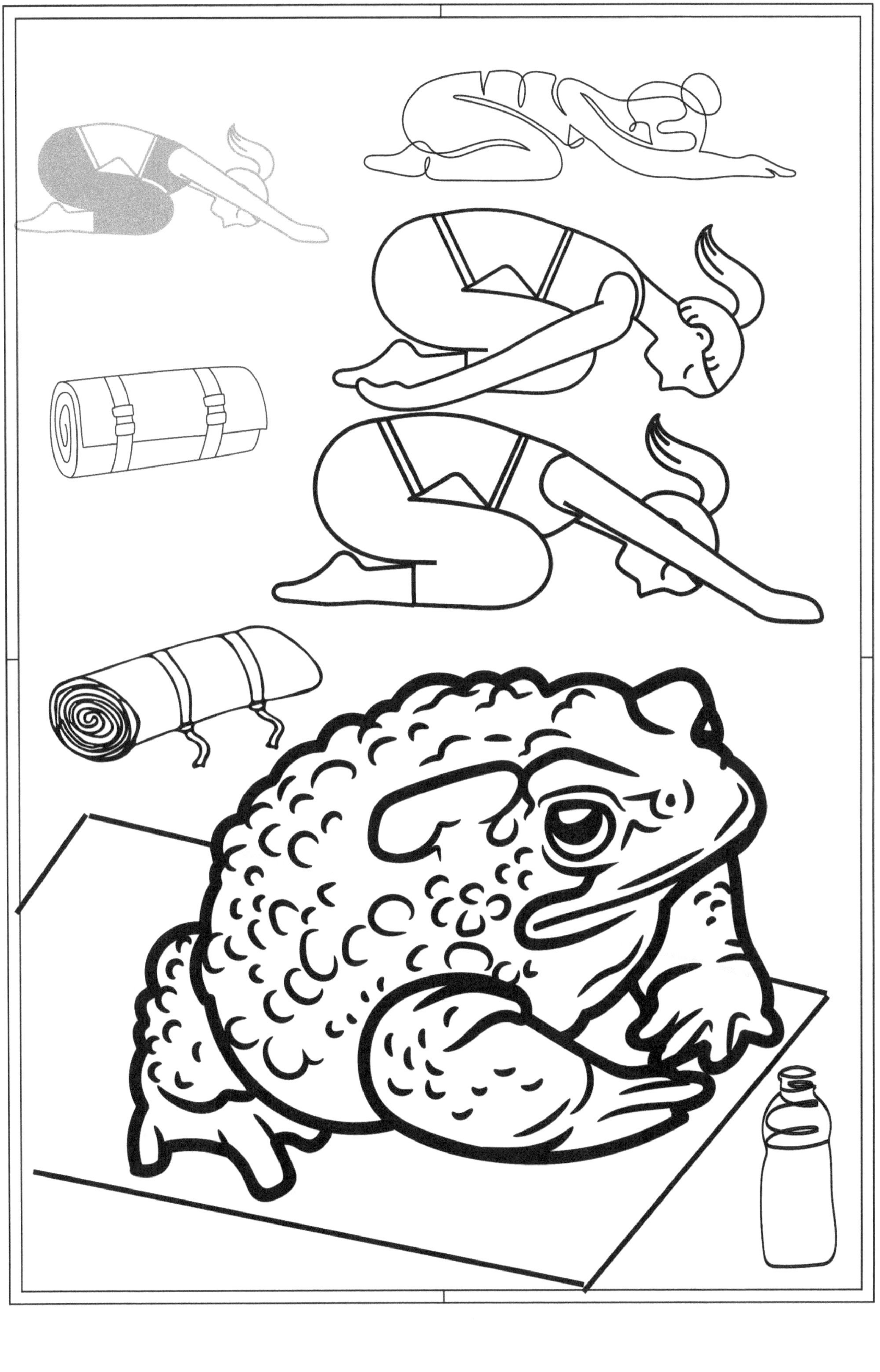

THANKS FOR COMING ALONG!

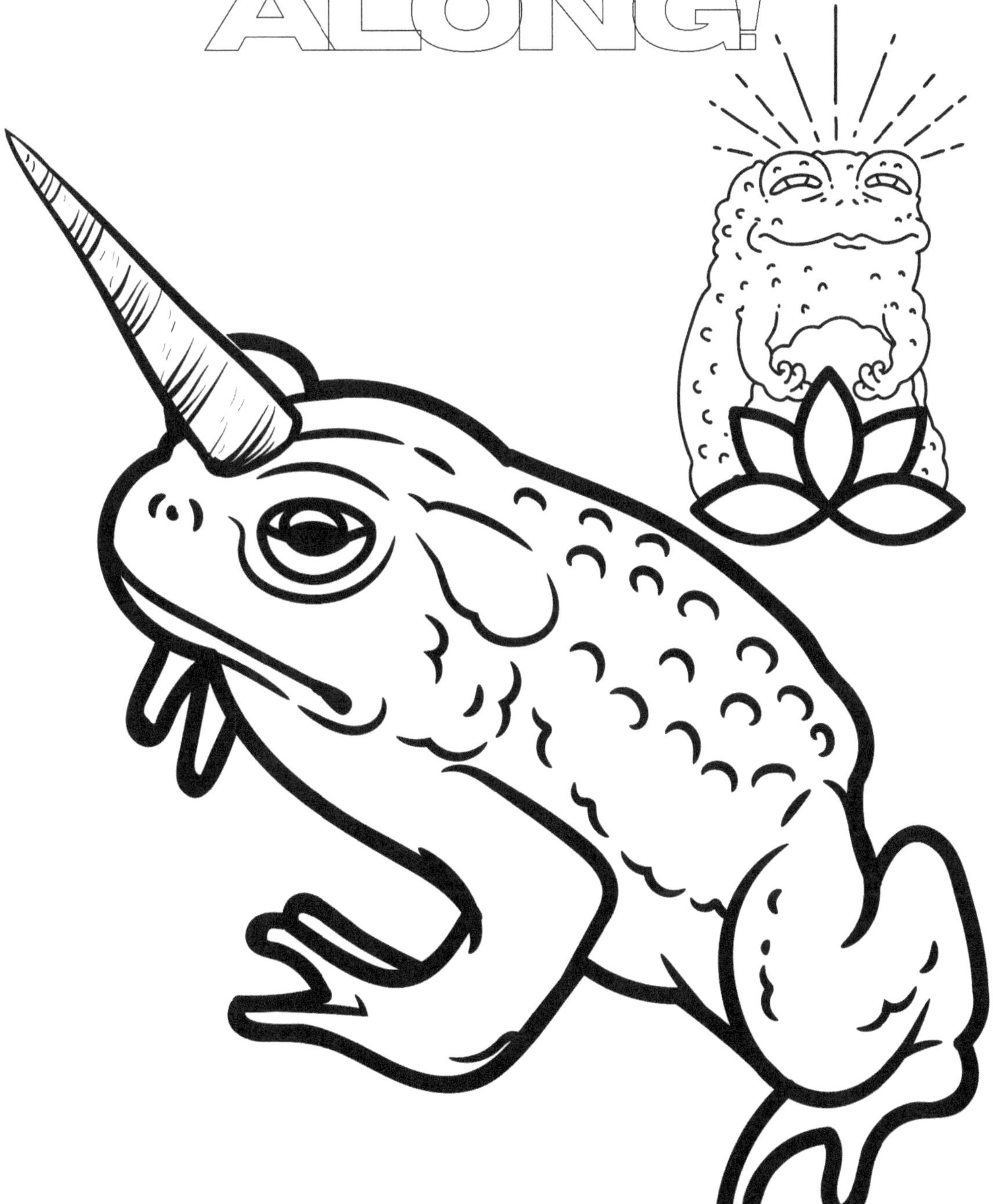

www.ingramcontent.com/pod-product-compliance
Lightning Source LLC
Chambersburg PA
CBHW080534220526
45465CB00006B/2706

* 9 7 9 8 3 5 5 8 2 8 5 4 7 *